Mastering Forex Trading: A Comprehensive Guide to Currency Trading Strategies and Risk Management

BY SIBUSISO NSIBANDE

This book is dedicated to my beloved 2-year-old son, who brings joy and inspiration to my life every day. May this guide serve as a testament to my love for you and a symbol of my commitment to providing for your future. I hope that one day you will find this book a useful resource as you navigate the world of finance and pursue your own dreams and aspirations.

Table of Contents

INTRODUCTION

Welcome to "Mastering Forex Trading: A Comprehensive Guide to Currency Trading Strategies and Risk Management." This guide is designed to provide aspiring forex traders with a comprehensive introduction to the world of forex trading, from the basics of currency pairs and market analysis to risk management and trading strategies.

Forex trading is a dynamic and exciting field that offers opportunities for financial freedom and independence. However, it is also a complex and risky field that requires discipline, patience, and a long-term perspective. The purpose of this guide is to provide traders with the knowledge and skills they need to succeed in this challenging but rewarding market.

Throughout this guide, you will learn about the different types of currency pairs and how to analyze them effectively, the importance of choosing a reliable forex broker, the different types of trading platforms available, and the key principles of effective risk management. You will also learn about various trading strategies, including fundamental analysis, technical analysis, and automated trading systems.

Whether you are a complete beginner or an experienced trader looking to improve your skills and knowledge, this guide will provide you with valuable insights and practical tips to help you succeed in the forex market. By approaching forex trading with discipline, patience, and a long-term perspective, traders can increase their chances of success and achieve their financial goals.

So let's dive in and explore the exciting world of forex trading together!

Chapter 1:

Introduction to Forex Trading

Forex trading, also known as foreign exchange trading, is the buying and selling of currencies in the foreign exchange market. The forex market is the largest financial market in the world, with an average daily turnover of over $6 trillion.

Benefits of Forex Trading

High liquidity: The forex market is highly liquid, meaning that there are always buyers and sellers available to trade with.

Accessibility: Anyone with an internet connection can trade forex, making it a highly accessible market.

Leverage: Forex brokers offer leverage, which allows traders to control large positions with a small amount of capital.

Diversification: Forex trading offers the opportunity to diversify an investment portfolio, as it is a market that operates independently of other financial markets.

Risks of Forex Trading

High volatility: The forex market is highly volatile, with currency prices fluctuating rapidly and often unpredictably.

Leverage: While leverage can increase potential profits, it can also increase potential losses, making risk management crucial in forex trading.

Complex market: The forex market can be complex and difficult to understand, requiring traders to have a solid understanding of market mechanics and trading strategies.

Overview of the Guide

This guide aims to provide beginners with a comprehensive introduction to forex trading. It will cover basic forex trading concepts, getting started with forex trading, developing a trading plan, trading strategies, risk management techniques, advanced forex trading concepts, and more. By the end of this guide, readers should have a solid understanding of forex trading and the tools and strategies needed to trade successfully.

Chapter 2:

Basic Forex Trading Concepts

Before diving into forex trading, it's important to have a solid understanding of some basic forex trading concepts. This chapter will cover the following topics:

- Understanding currency pairs
- Bid and ask prices
- Spreads
- Pips
- Leverage and margin
- Understanding risk management
- Understanding Currency Pairs

In forex trading, currencies are always traded in pairs. The first currency in the pair is called the base currency, while the second currency is called the quote currency. For example, in the

EUR/USD currency pair, the euro is the base currency and the US dollar is the quote currency.

Bid and Ask Prices

When trading forex, there are two prices to consider: the bid price and the ask price. The bid price is the price at which a trader can sell the base currency, while the ask price is the price at which a trader can buy the base currency. The difference between the bid and ask price is known as the spread.

Spreads

The spread is the difference between the bid and ask price and is measured in pips. Spreads can vary depending on the currency pair being traded and the broker being used. Generally, major currency pairs have tighter spreads, while exotic currency pairs have wider spreads.

Pips

Pips are the smallest unit of measurement in the forex market and are used to measure the change in price between two currencies. Most currency pairs are quoted to four decimal places, with the exception of the Japanese yen pairs, which are quoted to two decimal places. For example, if the EUR/USD currency pair moves from 1.2000 to 1.2005, it has moved 5 pips.

Leverage and Margin

Forex brokers offer leverage, which allows traders to control large positions with a small amount of capital. For example, with a leverage ratio of 1:100, a trader can control a position worth $100,000 with a margin requirement of $1,000. Margin is the amount of money required to open a leveraged position.

Understanding Risk Management

Risk management is crucial in forex trading, as the market is highly volatile and can result in significant losses if not managed properly. Traders should have a solid understanding of risk management techniques, such as position sizing, stop-loss orders, and take-profit orders, to help minimize potential losses. It's also important to have a trading plan in place and to stick to it, as well as to manage emotions while trading.

Chapter 3:

Getting Started with Forex Trading

Before starting to trade forex, it's important to choose a broker, set up a demo account, and familiarize yourself with trading platforms and basic analysis tools. This chapter will cover the following topics:

- Choosing a broker
- Setting up a demo account
- Understanding trading platforms
- Basic technical analysis tools
- Basic fundamental analysis tools
- Choosing a Broker

Choosing the right forex broker is crucial for success in forex trading. When selecting a broker, some factors to consider include:

Regulation: Make sure the broker is regulated by a reputable financial authority, such as the Financial Conduct Authority (FCA) in the UK or the National Futures Association (NFA) in the US.

Trading platforms: Ensure that the broker offers a trading platform that is user-friendly and suits your trading style.

Spreads and commissions: Look for a broker that offers competitive spreads and low commissions.

Deposit and withdrawal methods: Check that the broker offers convenient deposit and withdrawal methods that are accessible in your country.

Customer support: Ensure that the broker provides reliable and helpful customer support.

Setting up a Demo Account

Before trading with real money, it's recommended to set up a demo account with your chosen broker. A demo account allows you to practice trading in a risk-free environment, using virtual funds. This allows you to get familiar with the trading platform, test out trading strategies, and build confidence before trading with real money.

Understanding Trading Platforms

Most forex brokers offer trading platforms that allow traders to access the forex market. These platforms can vary in features and functionality, but typically include features such as:

- Charting tools and technical indicators
- News and market analysis
- Order management tools
- Risk management tools
- Trade execution tools
- Basic Technical Analysis Tools

Technical analysis involves analyzing price charts to identify patterns and trends that can help predict future price movements. Some basic technical analysis tools include:

- Support and resistance levels
- Moving averages
- Relative Strength Index (RSI)
- Moving Average Convergence Divergence (MACD)
- Bollinger Bands

Basic Fundamental Analysis Tools

Fundamental analysis involves analyzing economic and geopolitical events to determine their impact on the forex market. Some basic fundamental analysis tools include:

- Economic calendars
- Central bank announcements and policy decisions
- Political events and developments
- Market sentiment indicators

By familiarizing yourself with trading platforms and basic analysis tools, you'll be better equipped to make informed trading decisions and improve your chances of success in forex trading.

Chapter 4:

Developing a Forex Trading Strategy

A trading strategy is a set of rules that a trader uses to make trading decisions in the forex market. A well-defined and tested trading strategy can help improve trading results and minimize risk. This chapter will cover the following topics:

- Understanding trading styles
- Defining trading goals
- Choosing a trading approach
- Components of a trading strategy
- Backtesting and refining a strategy
- Understanding Trading Styles

There are different trading styles that traders can adopt, including:

Day trading: Traders buy and sell currencies within the same day, aiming to take advantage of short-term price movements.

Swing trading: Traders hold positions for several days to take advantage of medium-term price movements.

Position trading: Traders hold positions for several weeks or months to take advantage of long-term price movements.

Scalping: Traders aim to make small profits on many trades within a short period, typically using high leverage.

Defining Trading Goals

Before developing a trading strategy, it's important to define your trading goals. This can include factors such as the amount of capital you want to invest, your risk tolerance, and your desired return on investment.

Choosing a Trading Approach

Traders can use different approaches to develop a trading strategy, including:

Technical analysis: Traders use price charts and technical indicators to identify trading opportunities.

Fundamental analysis: Traders analyze economic and geopolitical events to identify trading opportunities.

Quantitative analysis: Traders use mathematical and statistical models to identify trading opportunities.

Algorithmic trading: Traders use computer programs to automatically execute trades based on predefined rules.

Components of a Trading Strategy

A trading strategy should include the following components:

Entry and exit rules: Define when to enter and exit trades based on your chosen approach.

Risk management rules: Define how much risk to take on each trade and how to manage risk through the use of stop-loss and take-profit orders.

Position sizing rules: Define how much capital to allocate to each trade based on your risk tolerance and account balance.

Trading plan: Define your overall trading plan, including trading hours, markets to trade, and trading goals.

Backtesting and Refining a Strategy

Once a trading strategy has been developed, it's important to test it using historical price data. This is known as backtesting and can help identify potential flaws in the strategy. Based on the results of backtesting, the strategy can be refined and adjusted to improve performance.

By following these steps, traders can develop a trading strategy that fits their trading style and goals, and increase their chances of success in the forex market

Chapter 5:

Managing Risk in Forex Trading

Forex trading involves a high level of risk, and it's important for traders to manage risk to protect their capital and maximize their returns. This chapter will cover the following topics:

- Understanding risk in forex trading
- Using stop-loss orders
- Using take-profit orders
- Managing leverage
- Diversifying your portfolio
- Developing a risk management plan
- Understanding Risk in Forex Trading

Forex trading involves the risk of losing money, and traders need to understand the potential risks before entering the market. Some of the risks include:

Market risk: The risk that the market moves against your position, resulting in losses.

Liquidity risk: The risk of not being able to close a position due to lack of buyers or sellers in the market.

Credit risk: The risk of a broker defaulting or becoming insolvent.

Operational risk: The risk of losses due to technical glitches, system failures, or human error.

Using Stop-Loss Orders

Stop-loss orders are used to limit potential losses by automatically closing a position when the price reaches a certain level. Traders can set a stop-loss order when entering a trade, or adjust it later to manage risk.

Using Take-Profit Orders

Take-profit orders are used to lock in profits by automatically closing a position when the price reaches a certain level. Traders can set a take-profit order when entering a trade, or adjust it later to take advantage of price movements.

Managing Leverage

Leverage allows traders to control a large position with a small amount of capital, but it also increases the potential risk. Traders should use leverage carefully and only trade with money they can afford to lose.

Diversifying Your Portfolio

Diversification involves spreading risk across multiple markets or assets to reduce overall risk. Traders can diversify their portfolio by trading multiple currency pairs, or by investing in other asset classes such as stocks, bonds, or commodities.

Developing a Risk Management Plan

A risk management plan should include the following:

Risk tolerance: Define your maximum acceptable level of risk.

Risk-reward ratio: Define the ratio of potential reward to potential risk for each trade.

Stop-loss and take-profit orders: Define the levels at which to close a position to limit potential losses and lock in profits.

Position sizing: Define the amount of capital to allocate to each trade based on your risk tolerance and account balance.

Portfolio diversification: Define how to diversify your portfolio to reduce overall risk.

By managing risk effectively, traders can protect their capital and increase their chances of success in the forex market.

Chapter 6:

Choosing a Forex Broker

Choosing the right forex broker is essential for success in the forex market. A broker acts as an intermediary between the trader and the market, and provides access to trading platforms, market data, and other tools. This chapter will cover the following topics:

- Understanding the role of a forex broker
- Regulatory considerations
- Trading platforms and tools
- Trading costs and fees
- Customer service and support
- Choosing the right broker for your needs
- Understanding the Role of a Forex Broker

A forex broker is a company that provides traders with access to the forex market. Brokers act as intermediaries between traders and the market, and provide trading platforms, market data, and other tools to help traders make informed trading decisions.

Regulatory Considerations

Regulation is an important consideration when choosing a forex broker. Regulated brokers are subject to oversight by regulatory bodies, which helps protect traders from fraud and other unethical practices. Traders should choose a broker that is regulated by a reputable regulatory body, such as the Financial Conduct Authority (FCA) in the UK or the National Futures Association (NFA) in the US.

Trading Platforms and Tools

Trading platforms and tools are important considerations when choosing a forex broker. A good trading platform should be easy to use, provide access to market data and analysis tools, and offer a range of order types and execution methods. Some brokers also offer mobile trading platforms, which allow traders to trade on the go.

Trading Costs and Fees

Trading costs and fees can vary widely between brokers, and can have a significant impact on trading profitability. Traders should consider factors such as spreads, commissions, and overnight financing charges when choosing a broker.

Customer Service and Support

Good customer service and support are important considerations when choosing a forex broker. Traders should choose a broker that offers prompt and efficient customer support, and provides a range of support options such as email, phone, and live chat.

Choosing the Right Broker for Your Needs

When choosing a forex broker, it's important to consider your individual needs and preferences. Traders should consider factors such as their trading style, account size, and trading goals when choosing a broker.

By choosing the right forex broker, traders can access the tools and resources they need to succeed in the forex market, and increase their chances of success.

Chapter 7:

Developing a Forex Trading Strategy

Developing a forex trading strategy is essential for success in the forex market. A trading strategy is a set of rules and guidelines that a trader follows to make trading decisions. This chapter will cover the following topics:

- Understanding the importance of a trading strategy
- Types of trading strategies
- Elements of a trading strategy
- Backtesting and optimization
- Risk management and trade management
- Implementing and refining your trading strategy

Understanding the Importance of a Trading Strategy

A trading strategy is essential for success in the forex market. A trading strategy provides a framework for making trading decisions, and helps traders to make consistent and objective decisions based on predefined rules.

Types of Trading Strategies

There are many different types of trading strategies, including:

Trend-following strategies: These strategies aim to identify and follow trends in the market.

Range trading strategies: These strategies aim to identify and trade within a range-bound market.

Breakout strategies: These strategies aim to identify and trade breakouts from key levels of support or resistance.

News trading strategies: These strategies aim to take advantage of market-moving news events.

Elements of a Trading Strategy

A trading strategy typically includes the following elements:

Entry criteria: The rules for entering a trade, such as identifying a trend or a breakout.

Exit criteria: The rules for exiting a trade, such as setting stop-loss and take-profit orders.

Position sizing: The rules for determining the size of each trade based on risk tolerance and account balance.

Risk management: The rules for managing risk, such as setting stop-loss orders and limiting leverage.

Trade management: The rules for managing open trades, such as adjusting stop-loss and take-profit orders as the trade progresses.

Backtesting and Optimization

Backtesting and optimization are important steps in developing a trading strategy. Backtesting involves testing a trading strategy using historical market data to see how it would have performed in the past. Optimization involves adjusting the strategy parameters to improve performance.

Risk Management and Trade Management

Risk management and trade management are important components of a trading strategy. Traders should use stop-loss orders to limit potential losses, and should adjust their position sizes based on their risk tolerance and account balance.

Implementing and Refining Your Trading Strategy

Once a trading strategy has been developed, it's important to implement it consistently and objectively. Traders should monitor their performance and refine their strategy as needed based on their results.

By developing a trading strategy and following it consistently, traders can increase their chances of success in the forex market.

Chapter 8:

Psychology of Forex Trading

The psychology of forex trading is an often overlooked but essential aspect of becoming a successful trader. The way a trader thinks, feels, and acts while trading can have a significant impact on their performance. This chapter will cover the following topics:

Understanding the importance of psychology in forex trading

- Common psychological traps in trading
- Managing emotions while trading
- Building a positive trading mindset
- Practicing self-discipline and staying focused
- Understanding the Importance of Psychology in Forex Trading

Psychology plays a crucial role in forex trading. Traders must be able to control their emotions, stick to their trading plan, and make objective decisions based on market analysis. Failing to do so can lead to costly mistakes and trading losses.

Common Psychological Traps in Trading

There are several common psychological traps that traders can fall into, including:

Overconfidence: Feeling invincible after a few successful trades.

Fear: Being afraid to enter or exit a trade.

Greed: Being driven by the desire to make more money, even if it means taking on unnecessary risk.

Revenge trading: Taking revenge on the market after a losing trade by making impulsive and emotional trades.

Managing Emotions While Trading

Managing emotions while trading is essential for success in the forex market. Traders should:

- Stay calm and avoid making impulsive decisions based on emotions.
- Stick to their trading plan and avoid making emotional decisions.
- Take breaks and step away from the computer if feeling overwhelmed.
- Building a Positive Trading Mindset

Building a positive trading mindset involves:

- Focusing on the process rather than the outcome.
- Accepting losses as part of the trading process.
- Practicing self-reflection and learning from mistakes.

- Practicing Self-Discipline and Staying Focused
- Practicing self-discipline and staying focused is essential for success in the forex market. Traders should:
- Create a trading plan and stick to it.
- Avoid distractions and focus on the task at hand.
- Practice self-control and avoid making impulsive decisions.

By understanding the importance of psychology in forex trading, traders can learn to manage their emotions, build a positive trading mindset, and practice self-discipline and focus. These skills can help traders become more successful in the forex market.

Chapter 9:

Resources for Forex Trading

There are many resources available for forex traders to help them learn and improve their trading skills. This chapter will cover the following topics:

- Educational resources for forex trading
- Trading platforms and tools
- News and analysis resources
- Online communities and forums
- Trading psychology resources
- Educational Resources for Forex Trading
- There are many educational resources available for forex traders, including:

Online courses and tutorials: Many websites offer free and paid courses and tutorials on forex trading, ranging from beginner to advanced levels.

Books: There are many books available on forex trading, covering topics such as technical analysis, fundamental analysis, and trading psychology.

Webinars and seminars: Many forex brokers and trading platforms offer free webinars and seminars on forex trading topics.

Trading academies: Some forex brokers offer trading academies, which are educational programs designed to teach traders about forex trading.

Trading Platforms and Tools

Trading platforms and tools are essential for forex traders. Some popular trading platforms and tools include:

MetaTrader 4 and 5: MetaTrader is a popular trading platform used by many forex brokers. It offers a range of features, including technical analysis tools, customizable charts, and automated trading.

TradingView: TradingView is a web-based charting platform that offers a range of technical analysis tools and features, including customizable charts and social trading.

Forex robots: Forex robots are automated trading systems that can analyze the market and make trades on behalf of the trader.

News and Analysis Resources

Staying up-to-date with the latest news and analysis is important for forex traders. Some popular news and analysis resources include:

Forex news websites: There are many websites that offer forex news and analysis, including Forex Factory, FXStreet, and Investing.com.

Economic calendars: Economic calendars provide information on upcoming economic events and their potential impact on the market.

Market analysis tools: Some forex brokers and trading platforms offer market analysis tools, such as sentiment indicators and market news feeds.

Online Communities and Forums

Online communities and forums are a great way for forex traders to connect with other traders and share ideas and experiences. Some popular online communities and forums include:

Forex Factory: Forex Factory is a popular online community for forex traders. It offers a range of features, including a forum, economic calendar, and market news feed.

Reddit: The forex subreddit is a community of forex traders who share news, analysis, and trading ideas.

TradingView: TradingView offers a social trading community where traders can share ideas and analysis.

Trading Psychology Resources

Managing emotions and developing a positive trading mindset is essential for forex traders. Some popular trading psychology resources include:

Trading psychology books: There are many books available on trading psychology, covering topics such as risk management, emotional control, and discipline.

Trading psychology coaches: Some trading coaches specialize in trading psychology and can help traders develop a positive mindset and manage their emotions.

Meditation and mindfulness practices: Some traders find that meditation and mindfulness practices can help them stay focused and manage their emotions while trading.

By taking advantage of the many resources available for forex traders, traders can improve their skills, stay up-to-date with the latest news and analysis, and develop a positive trading mindset.

Chapter 10:

Risks and Rewards of Forex Trading

Forex trading is a popular way to invest and make money, but it is important to understand the risks and rewards involved. In this chapter, we will discuss the following topics:

- Risks of forex trading
- Rewards of forex trading
- Managing risks in forex trading
- Balancing risk and reward in forex trading
- Risks of Forex Trading
- Forex trading involves several risks, including:

Market risk: Forex prices can be volatile and change rapidly due to factors such as economic events, political events, and market sentiment.

Leverage risk: Forex trading typically involves leverage, which means that traders can control large positions with a small amount of capital. While leverage can increase profits, it can also amplify losses.

Counterparty risk: Forex trading involves trading with a counterparty, which can include a forex broker or other traders. There is a risk that the counterparty may not fulfill their obligations.

Operational risk: Forex trading can involve technical issues, such as platform failures or internet connection problems, which can affect trading results.

Rewards of Forex Trading

Forex trading also offers several rewards, including:

High liquidity: The forex market is the largest financial market in the world, with high levels of liquidity that allow traders to buy and sell currencies quickly and easily.

24-hour trading: The forex market is open 24 hours a day, five days a week, and allowing traders to trade at any time.

Potential for high returns: Forex trading offers the potential for high returns, especially when using leverage.

Diversification: Forex trading allows traders to diversify their investment portfolios and hedge against other investments.

Managing Risks in Forex Trading

To manage risks in forex trading, traders should:

Use risk management tools: Forex brokers and trading platforms offer a range of risk management tools, such as stop-loss orders, limit orders, and trailing stops.

Set realistic goals: Traders should set realistic goals and avoid making trades based on emotion or greed.

Develop a trading plan: Traders should develop a trading plan that includes entry and exit points, risk management strategies, and trading goals.

Practice good money management: Traders should use good money management techniques, such as risk-to-reward ratios and proper position sizing.

Balancing Risk and Reward in Forex Trading

Balancing risk and reward in forex trading is essential for success. Traders should:

Understand their risk tolerance: Traders should understand their risk tolerance and avoid taking on too much risk.

Focus on risk-to-reward ratios: Traders should focus on trades that offer a favorable risk-to-reward ratio, which means that the potential reward is greater than the potential risk.

Use proper position sizing: Traders should use proper position sizing techniques to avoid taking on too much risk.

Stay disciplined: Traders should stay disciplined and stick to their trading plan, even in the face of losses or unexpected events.

In conclusion, forex trading offers the potential for high returns, but it is important to understand the risks involved and take steps to manage those risks. By balancing risk and reward, using risk management tools, and staying disciplined, traders can increase their chances of success in the forex market.

Chapter 11:

Choosing a Forex Broker

Choosing the right forex broker is crucial to successful trading. In this chapter, we will discuss the following topics:

What is a forex broker?

Factors to consider when choosing a forex broker

- Types of forex brokers
- Top forex brokers
- What is a Forex Broker?

A **forex broker** is a company that provides traders with access to the forex market. They typically offer trading platforms, educational resources, and other services to help traders make informed decisions.

Factors to Consider When Choosing a Forex Broker

When choosing a forex broker, it is important to consider the following factors:

Regulations: Choose a broker that is regulated by a reputable financial authority, such as the Financial Conduct Authority (FCA) in the UK or the Securities and Exchange Commission (SEC) in the US.

Trading platforms: Make sure the broker offers a trading platform that is user-friendly and has the features you need, such as charting tools and technical indicators.

Customer support: Choose a broker that offers responsive customer support, preferably 24/7.

Fees and commissions: Look for a broker that offers competitive fees and commissions, and be aware of any hidden costs.

Payment methods: Choose a broker that offers payment methods that are convenient and secure for you.

Educational resources: Look for a broker that offers educational resources, such as webinars, tutorials, and trading tools, to help you improve your trading skills.

Types of Forex Brokers

There are several types of forex brokers, including:

Market makers: Market makers provide liquidity by taking the other side of traders' trades. They typically offer fixed spreads and do not charge commissions.

ECN brokers: ECN brokers provide a marketplace where traders can buy and sell currencies directly with each other. They offer variable spreads and charge commissions.

STP brokers: STP brokers route traders' orders directly to liquidity providers, such as banks and other brokers. They offer variable spreads and may or may not charge commissions.

Top Forex Brokers

There are many forex brokers to choose from, but some of the top ones include:

IG: IG offers a range of trading platforms and educational resources, and is regulated by the FCA and other financial authorities.

Oanda: Oanda offers a user-friendly trading platform and competitive fees, and is regulated by the FCA and other financial authorities.

Forex.com: Forex.com offers a range of trading platforms and educational resources, and is regulated by the FCA and other financial authorities.

eToro: eToro offers a social trading platform that allows traders to copy the trades of successful traders, and is regulated by the FCA and other financial authorities.

In conclusion, choosing the right forex broker is crucial to successful trading. Traders should consider factors such as regulations, trading platforms, customer support, fees and commissions, payment methods, and educational resources when selecting a broker. They should also be aware of the different types of brokers, such as market makers, ECN brokers, and STP brokers, and choose the one that best suits their trading style and preferences.

Chapter 12:

Risk Management in Forex Trading

Forex trading can be a high-risk activity, but with proper risk management techniques, traders can minimize their losses and increase their chances of success. In this chapter, we will discuss the following topics:

- Importance of risk management in forex trading
- Risk management techniques
- Setting stop-loss orders
- Position sizing
- Diversification
- Importance of Risk Management in Forex Trading

Risk management is the process of identifying, analyzing, and mitigating potential risks. In forex trading, risk management is essential to protect your capital and avoid large losses. Without proper risk management techniques, traders may expose themselves to significant losses and potentially wipe out their trading account.

Risk Management Techniques

Here are some risk management techniques that traders can use in forex trading:

Setting Stop-Loss Orders

A stop-loss order is an order placed with a broker to sell a security when it reaches a certain price. It is a way to limit your losses by exiting a trade before it goes too far against you. Traders should set stop-loss orders on every trade to limit their potential losses.

Position Sizing

Position sizing refers to determining the amount of capital to risk on each trade. Traders should only risk a small percentage of their trading account on each trade, typically 1-2%. This ensures that losses on individual trades do not have a significant impact on the overall trading account.

Diversification

Diversification refers to spreading your investments across different asset classes or instruments to reduce risk. In forex trading, diversification can be achieved by trading multiple currency pairs or incorporating other financial instruments, such as stocks or commodities, into your portfolio.

In conclusion, risk management is an essential part of forex trading. Traders should use techniques such as setting stop-loss orders, position sizing, and diversification to protect their capital and minimize their losses. By practicing good risk management, traders can increase their chances of success and achieve their trading goals

Chapter 13:

Developing a Forex Trading Plan

A trading plan is a comprehensive document that outlines a trader's goals, strategies, and risk management techniques. In forex trading, a trading plan is essential to ensure consistent profits and minimize losses. In this chapter, we will discuss the following topics:

- Importance of a trading plan
- Components of a trading plan
- Developing a trading strategy
- Implementing risk management techniques
- Reviewing and updating your trading plan
- Importance of a Trading Plan

A **trading plan** is crucial in forex trading as it provides a framework for making trading decisions. It helps traders to stay disciplined and avoid emotional trading decisions that can lead to losses. A well-crafted trading plan can also help traders to stay focused on their goals and minimize the impact of market volatility.

Components of a Trading Plan

A trading plan should include the following components:

Trading Goals - Define your trading goals, such as the desired level of profit, trading frequency, and risk tolerance.

Trading Strategy - Develop a trading strategy based on technical and fundamental analysis, including the identification of key entry and exit points.

Risk Management - Implement risk management techniques, such as position sizing, stop-loss orders, and diversification.

Trading Schedule - Establish a trading schedule, including the best time to trade, the number of trades per day or week, and the amount of time to be spent on analysis and research.

Trading Journal - Keep a trading journal to record your trades, including the entry and exit points, the reasons for the trade, and the outcome.

Developing a Trading Strategy

A trading strategy is a set of rules that govern when and how to enter and exit trades. To develop a trading strategy, traders should consider factors such as market conditions, technical indicators, and economic news. Traders should also test their trading strategies using historical data to determine their effectiveness.

Implementing Risk Management Techniques

Risk management is an essential component of a trading plan. Traders should use risk management techniques such as position sizing, stop-loss orders, and diversification to manage their risk exposure and protect their capital.

Reviewing and Updating Your Trading Plan

A trading plan is not a static document and should be reviewed and updated regularly to reflect changes in market conditions, trading goals, and risk tolerance. Traders should also analyze their trading performance regularly and make adjustments to their trading plan as necessary.

In conclusion, a trading plan is essential for successful forex trading. Traders should develop a comprehensive trading plan that includes clear goals, a well-defined trading strategy, and effective risk management techniques. By sticking to their trading plan, traders can minimize losses and achieve consistent profits over time.

Chapter 14:

Candlestick Patterns in Forex Trading

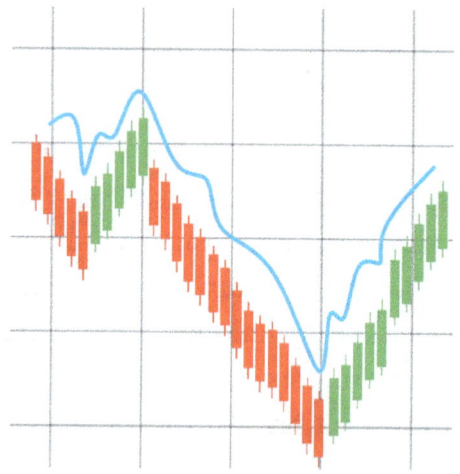

Candlestick charts are a popular tool used in forex trading to analyze price movements and identify potential trading opportunities. Candlestick patterns can provide traders with valuable insights into market sentiment and help them make informed trading decisions. In this chapter, we will discuss the following topics:

- What are candlestick charts?
- Basic candlestick patterns
- Advanced candlestick patterns
- How to use candlestick patterns in forex trading
- What are Candlestick Charts?

Candlestick charts are a type of chart used in technical analysis to track the price movements of an asset, such as a currency pair. Candlestick charts provide traders with information on the opening, closing, high, and low prices of an asset over a specific period.

Candlestick charts are made up of individual candles, which represent a specific time period, such as one hour, one day, or one week. Each candle has a body, which represents the opening and closing prices, and wicks, which represent the high and low prices.

Basic Candlestick Patterns

There are several basic candlestick patterns that traders use to analyze price movements and identify potential trading opportunities. These include:

Doji: A Doji candlestick pattern occurs when the opening and closing prices are the same or very close, and the wicks are long. This pattern indicates indecision in the market and can signal a potential reversal.

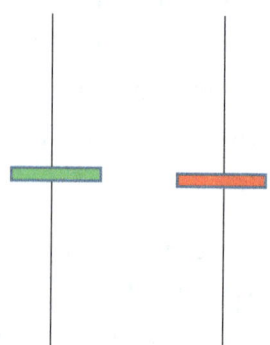

Figure 1 Doji Candlestick

Hammer: A Hammer candlestick pattern occurs when the opening and closing prices are near the high of the candle, and the wick is long. This pattern can indicate a potential bullish reversal.

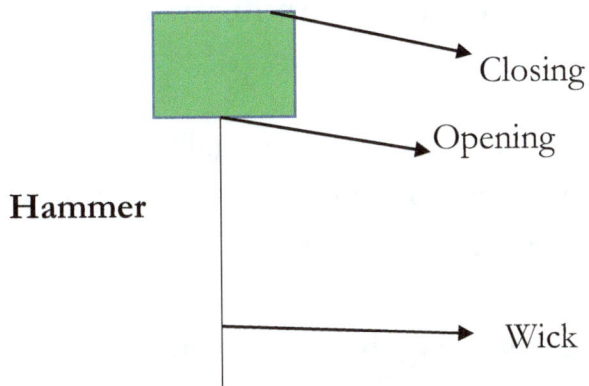

Closing

Opening

Hammer

Wick

Figure 2 Hammer candle stick

Shooting star: A Shooting Star candlestick pattern occurs when the opening and closing prices are near the low of the candle, and the wick is long. This pattern can indicate a potential bearish reversal.

Figure 3 Shooting star

Advanced Candlestick Patterns

There are also advanced candlestick patterns that traders use to analyze price movements and identify potential trading opportunities. These include:

Bullish engulfing: A Bullish Engulfing candlestick pattern occurs when a small bearish candle is followed by a large bullish candle that completely engulfs the previous candle. This pattern can indicate a potential bullish reversal.

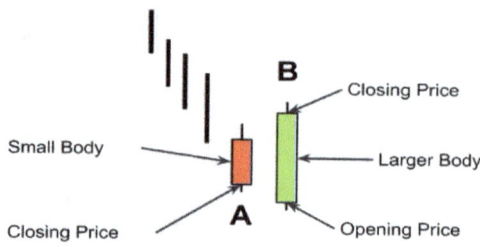

Figure 4 Bullish engulfing

Bearish engulfing: A Bearish Engulfing candlestick pattern occurs when a small bullish candle is followed by a large bearish candle that completely engulfs the previous candle. This pattern can indicate a potential bearish reversal.

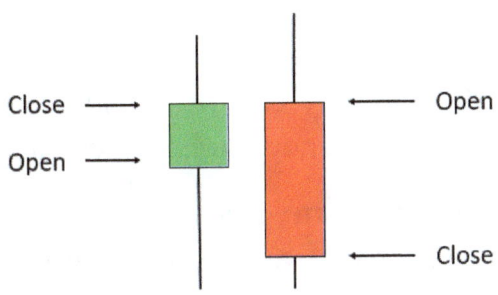

Figure 5 Bearish engulfing

Three white soldiers: A Three White Soldiers candlestick pattern occurs when three consecutive bullish candles are formed with each candle closing higher than the previous candle. This pattern can indicate a potential bullish trend continuation.

Figure 6 Three white soldiers

How to Use Candlestick Patterns in Forex Trading

Traders can use candlestick patterns to analyze price movements and identify potential trading opportunities. To use candlestick patterns effectively, traders should follow these steps:

Identify the pattern: Traders should be able to identify different candlestick patterns and understand what they indicate about market sentiment.

Confirm the pattern: Traders should confirm the candlestick pattern by analyzing other technical indicators and market data.

Enter the trade: Traders should enter the trade after confirming the pattern and implementing an effective risk management strategy.

In conclusion, candlestick patterns are a valuable tool used by forex traders to analyze price movements and identify potential trading opportunities. Traders should be able to identify different candlestick patterns and understand what they indicate about market sentiment. By confirming the pattern and implementing an effective risk management strategy, traders can use candlestick patterns to make informed trading decisions.

Chapter 15:

Forex Entries

Forex entries refer to the point at which a trader opens a position in the market. Entering a trade at the right time can determine the success of a trader. In this chapter, we will discuss the following topics:

- Different types of forex entries
- Factors to consider before entering a trade
- Tips for effective forex entries
- Different Types of Forex Entries

There are several types of forex entries that traders can use to enter a trade. These include:

Market order: A market order is an order to buy or sell a currency pair at the current market price. This is the most common type of entry and is used when a trader wants to enter a trade immediately.

Limit order: A limit order is an order to buy or sell a currency pair at a specific price. This type of entry is used when a trader wants to enter a trade at a specific price.

Stop order: A stop order is an order to buy or sell a currency pair at a specific price. This type of entry is used when a trader wants to enter a trade when the market moves in a certain direction.

Factors to Consider Before Entering a Trade

Before entering a trade, traders should consider the following factors:

Market conditions: Traders should analyze market conditions to determine the best time to enter a trade. This includes analyzing fundamental and technical factors that affect currency prices.

Risk management: Traders should implement proper risk management strategies to minimize losses and protect their capital.

Trading plan: Traders should have a clear trading plan that outlines their entry and exit strategies, as well as their risk management strategies.

Tips for Effective Forex Entries

To enter a trade effectively, traders should follow these tips:

Wait for confirmation: Traders should wait for confirmation of a trend before entering a trade. This can be done by analyzing technical indicators and market conditions.

Use stop-loss orders: Traders should use stop-loss orders to minimize losses and protect their capital.

Monitor the trade: Traders should monitor their trades and adjust their positions as market conditions change.

Be patient: Traders should be patient and wait for the right opportunity to enter a trade. Rushing into a trade can lead to losses and missed opportunities.

Chapter 16:

Managing Your Capital

Managing your capital is crucial to long-term success in forex trading. In this chapter, we will discuss the following topics:

- The importance of capital management
- Different strategies for managing your capital
- Tips for effective capital management
- The Importance of Capital Management

Capital management refers to the process of allocating your funds in a way that maximizes your returns while minimizing your risk exposure. The main goal of capital management is to protect your trading capital and grow it over time. Proper capital management can help you avoid common pitfalls such as overtrading and emotional decision-making, which can lead to significant losses.

Different Strategies for Managing Your Capital

There are several strategies that traders use for managing their capital, including:

Risk-to-reward ratio: This strategy involves setting a risk-to-reward ratio for each trade. This ratio determines the amount of potential profit compared to the amount of potential loss. For example, a trader might set a risk-to-reward ratio of 1:2, meaning that they are willing to risk $1 to make $2.

Position sizing: This strategy involves adjusting the size of your position based on the amount of capital you have available and the level of risk involved in the trade. Traders might use a fixed percentage of their account balance for each trade or adjust their position size based on the volatility of the market.

Stop-loss orders: This strategy involves setting stop-loss orders to limit your losses in case the market moves against you. Traders might use a fixed dollar amount or a percentage of their account balance as their stop-loss level.

Tips for Effective Capital Management

To manage your capital effectively, consider these tips:

Set realistic goals: Set realistic goals for your trading and adjust your strategy accordingly. This will help you avoid overtrading and making emotional decisions.

Monitor your risk exposure: Monitor your risk exposure and adjust your position size and risk-to-reward ratio accordingly.

Use stop-loss orders: Always use stop-loss orders to limit your losses and protect your capital.

Avoid overtrading: Avoid overtrading and stick to your trading plan.

Diversify your portfolio: Diversify your portfolio by trading different currency pairs and using different strategies.

Stay disciplined: Stay disciplined and avoid making impulsive decisions based on emotions. Stick to your trading plan and adjust it as necessary based on market conditions.

Proper capital management is essential for success in forex trading. By using the right strategies and following these tips, you can protect your capital and grow it over time.

Chapter 17:

Forex Trading Strategies

Forex trading strategies are a set of rules and techniques used by traders to make trading decisions. In this chapter, we will discuss the following topics:

- Types of forex trading strategies
- Technical analysis strategies
- Fundamental analysis strategies
- Risk management strategies
- Developing your own forex trading strategy
- Types of Forex Trading Strategies

There are two main types of forex trading strategies: technical analysis strategies and fundamental analysis strategies.

Technical analysis strategies: These strategies rely on analyzing past market data to identify trends and patterns that can be used to predict future price movements. Technical traders use a variety of tools and indicators, such as moving averages, support and resistance levels, and chart patterns, to make trading decisions.

Fundamental analysis strategies: These strategies rely on analyzing economic, financial, and geopolitical events and their impact on currency prices. Fundamental traders focus on factors such as interest rates, inflation, employment, and political events to make trading decisions.

Technical Analysis Strategies

Technical analysis strategies are based on the idea that historical price and volume data can be used to predict future price movements. Some common technical analysis strategies include:

Moving averages: This strategy involves using moving averages to identify trends in the market. Traders might use simple moving averages, such as the 50-day or 200-day moving average, or exponential moving averages, which give more weight to recent price data.

Support and resistance levels: This strategy involves identifying key levels of support and resistance on a chart. Support levels are areas where buying pressure is expected to be strong, while resistance levels are areas where selling pressure is expected to be strong.

Candlestick patterns: This strategy involves analyzing candlestick charts to identify patterns that can be used to predict future price movements. Common candlestick patterns include doji, hammer, and engulfing patterns.

Fundamental Analysis Strategies

Fundamental analysis strategies are based on the idea that economic, financial, and geopolitical events can impact currency prices. Some common fundamental analysis strategies include:

Interest rate differentials: This strategy involves comparing the interest rates of two currencies to predict future currency movements. Higher interest rates can attract investors and increase demand for a currency.

Economic indicators: This strategy involves analyzing economic indicators such as GDP, inflation, and employment data to make trading decisions. Strong economic data can lead to increased demand for a currency, while weak data can lead to decreased demand.

Risk Management Strategies

Risk management strategies are used to minimize potential losses and protect trading capital. Some common risk management strategies include:

Stop-loss orders: This strategy involves setting stop-loss orders to limit potential losses in case the market moves against you.

Position sizing: This strategy involves adjusting the size of your position based on the level of risk involved in the trade.

Risk-to-reward ratio: This strategy involves setting a risk-to-reward ratio for each trade to ensure that potential profits outweigh potential losses.

Developing Your Own Forex Trading Strategy

Developing your own forex trading strategy requires a combination of technical and fundamental analysis skills, as well as an understanding of risk management principles. To develop your own strategy, consider the following steps:

Identify your goals: Determine your trading goals, risk tolerance, and preferred trading style.

Learn the basics: Learn the basics of technical and fundamental analysis and risk management.

Test your strategy: Test your strategy using a demo account or backtesting software to see how it performs in different market conditions.

Refine your strategy: Refine your strategy based on your testing results and adjust it as necessary based on market conditions.

Stay disciplined: Stick to your trading plan and avoid making impulsive decisions based on emotions.

By developing your own forex trading strategy, you can tailor your approach to your own goals

Conclusion

Forex trading can be a highly lucrative opportunity for those who take the time to learn the ins and outs of the market. However, it is important to remember that forex trading carries risks and should not be entered into lightly. As with any type of investment or financial venture, it is important to approach forex trading with a long-term perspective, patience, and discipline.

One of the most important aspects of successful forex trading is developing a strong foundation of knowledge and skills. This includes understanding the basic concepts of currency pairs, market analysis, and trading strategies. In addition, it is important to choose a reliable and reputable forex broker, and to take the time to understand the different trading platforms available.

Effective risk management is also essential in forex trading. This includes setting realistic trading goals and limits, managing leverage, and using stop-loss orders to protect against unexpected market movements. By managing risk effectively, traders can limit their exposure to potential losses and preserve their capital over the long term.

Trading strategies are another key aspect of successful forex trading. There are many different approaches to trading, including fundamental analysis, technical analysis, and automated trading systems. Each approach has its own strengths and weaknesses, and it is important to choose a strategy that aligns with one's goals, risk tolerance, and trading style.

In conclusion, forex trading can be a challenging but rewarding venture for those who are willing to put in the time and effort to learn the fundamentals and develop effective trading strategies. By approaching forex trading with discipline, patience, and a long-term perspective, traders can increase their chances of success and achieve their financial goals.